Fire TV Stick Instructions
Fire TV Stick User Guide
By Emery H. Maxwell

Table of Contents

Welcome

Welcome to the *Fire TV Stick User Guide*. This manual is intended to help you install *Fire TV Stick* and explain how to get the most out of it.

It will cover:

- How to set up *Fire TV Stick*
- How to connect the device to the internet
- How to navigate
- How to power down the device and go back to watching regular TV
- How to use *ALEXA* Voice Remote
- How to save titles
- How to transfer media to external storage
- How to manage apps
- Troubleshooting

Getting Started

This section will go over the specifications of the device, how to set up *Fire Stick*, how to navigate, and how to power down the device and go back to watching regular TV.

Specifications

Fire TV Stick

Inside the Box: *Fire TV Stick, ALEXA Voice Remote*, USB cable and power adapter, 2 AAA batteries, quick start guide, HDMI extender.

Size: 3.4" x 1.2" x 0.5" (85.9 mm x 30 mm x 12.6 mm)

Weight: 1.1 oz (32 g)

Storage: 8 GB internal

Processor: MEDIATEK Quad-core ARM 1.3 GHZ

GPU: MALI450 MP4

Ports: HDMI output, Micro USB for power only

WI-FI connectivity: Dual-band, dual-antenna WI-FI supports 2x2 MIMO 802.11a/b/g/n/ac

BLUETOOTH: BLUETOOTH 4.1

Audio support: DOLBY Audio, 5.1 surround sound, 2ch stereo, and HDMI audio pass through up to 7.1

Cloud Storage: Free cloud storage for all *Amazon* content

Voice Support: Yes, optimized for *Amazon Fire TV* controller. Most games are compatible with other BLUETOOTH controllers.

System Requirements: High-def TV with available HDMI input, internet connection through WI-FI, a power outlet.

Output resolution supported: 720p and 1080p up to 60 FPS

Accessibility features: *VOICEVIEW screen reader* for users who are visually impaired, *Screen Magnifier*, closed captioning display. Captions are not available for all content, however.

ALEXA Voice Remote (2nd Generation)

*The *Fire TV Stick* Basic Edition does not include the *ALEXA* Voice Remote.

Size: 1.5" x 5.9" x 0.7" (38.4 mm x 150.7 mm x 16.7 mm

Weight: 2.4 oz (68 g) with batteries. 1.6 oz (45 g) without batteries.

Batteries: 2 AAA

How to Set up *Fire TV Stick*

1.) **Connect the power adapter**.

• Plug the small end of the USB cord into the Micro-USB port on the *Fire TV Stick*.

• Plug the other end into the power adapter.

• Plug the power adapter into the outlet.

Note: It is recommended that you use the included power adapter or HDMI extender when setting up the *Fire TV Stick*. This will ensure that the *Fire TV Stick* fits securely into the TV.

2.) **Connect to your compatible TV**

To meet compatibility requirements, the TV must be High-def or Ultra High-def. The TV must also have an HDMI input port.

• Plug the *Fire TV Stick* into an HDMI port on the TV.

3.) **Select the input channel**

• Power on the TV.

• Select the HDMI input channel for the port you used to connect the *Fire TV Stick*.

• You should then see a loading screen displaying the *Fire TV Stick* logo.

4.) **Set up the remote**

• Insert 2 AAA batteries into the remote.

Note: To remove the battery cover, use an upward motion to press where the arrow is pointing. After the cover slides up slightly, lift the back cover up and away from the remote. After inserting the batteries, reattach the cover by sliding it downward until it clicks into place.

5.) **Pair the remote**

• After inserting the batteries, the remote should pair with the *Fire TV Stick* automatically. But if it does not pair right away, press and hold the **Home** button for up to 10 seconds. This will send it into *discovery mode*, so the pairing process can be completed.

6.) **Connect to the internet**

• Follow the onscreen instructions.

<u>Connecting to WI-FI</u>

• Select **Settings > Network** from the *Fire TV* menu. The device detects nearby networks automatically.

• Select your network. If you don't see your network, select **RESCAN**. If you still don't see your network, select **Join Other Network**.

• If necessary, enter the WI-FI password.

Connecting a 2nd Generation *Fire TV Stick* to a wired network by using an *Amazon* Ethernet Adapter for *Amazon Fire TV* Devices (not included)

• Connect the *Amazon* Ethernet Adapter for *Amazon Fire TV* devices to the *Fire TV Stick's* USB port.

• Plug the USB power cable into the Ethernet adapter.

• Connect one end of the Ethernet cable to the back of the Ethernet adapter, then connect the other end to an Ethernet port on the router or modem.

• Select **Settings > Network** from the *Fire TV* menu.

• Select the **Wired** option.

7.) **Register the device**

If you purchased the device from the *Amazon* website, it should be registered automatically to the *Amazon* account you used to place your order.

To view or change the account your device is registered to from the *Settings menu*

• Select **Settings** from the *Fire TV* menu.

• Go to **My Account**.

If the device is registered, the name associated with the account will display in the **My Account** section.

If the device is not registered, a **Register** option will be displayed on the screen in the **My Account** section. Select **Register** and enter your account information when prompted to do so.

If the device was received as a gift, it might need to be unregistered and then registered again if the gift sender did not select *this is a gift* at checkout.

8.) **Watch the Welcome video**

How to Navigate

Home: Located near the center of the remote, this button will bring you to the Home screen.

Back: Located to the left of the *Home* button, pressing this button will bring you back to the previous screen.

Menu: Located to the right of the *Home* button, use this button to view more options. This button can also be used to see available viewing options when you have a movie or TV show highlighted.

Navigation (Directional Keypad): Allows you to scroll left, right, up, or down.

Select: Located at the center of the directional keypad, use this button to select your highlighted selection.

Voice: Located on top of the directional keypad, press and hold this button and simply say what you are searching for.

You can also search via text by selecting **Search** from the *Fire TV* menu.

Microphone: Located on top of the *Voice* button.

How to Restart, Shut down, and put the device to Sleep

Restart the Device

• Press and hold the **Select** and **Play/Pause** buttons at the same time for approximately five seconds.

Shut down the Device

• Simply unplug the power cord from the back of the device or the wall outlet.

Putting the Device into Sleep Mode

Although the *Fire TV* device automatically goes into sleep mode after 20-30 minutes of inactivity, it can also be sent into *Sleep* mode manually.

1.) Press and hold the **Home** button on the remote.

2.) Wait for the **Quick Access** menu to launch.

3.) Select the **Sleep** option.

<u>How to Use *ALEXA* Voice Remote</u>

To use the *ALEXA* Voice feature, press and hold the **Voice** button on the *ALEXA* Voice Remote or the *Fire TV* Remote app. Then ask *ALEXA* a question or give a command. *ALEXA* will respond via the *Fire TV*.

Below is a list of requests to give *ALEXA*.

<u>Search</u>

"Search for [title /genre / actor]."

"Search for [genre] with [actor]."

"Find the app [title]."

"Search for [title / actor / genre] on [app]."

<u>Movies and TV Shows</u>

"Watch [title]."

"Play [title] on [app]."

"Launch [app name]."

"Open [app name]."

"Go to [channel / network]."

"Go to [channel / network] on [app]."

"Rewind [number] minutes / fast forward [number] seconds / jump to [number] minutes."

"Next episode."

<u>Music</u>

"Play the [name] Prime Station."

"Play music by [artist]."

"Play my [artist name] station on *Prime Music*."

"Play my [artist name] station on *Amazon Music*."

"Next / Previous song."

"Buy this album/song."

<u>Audible and Digital Books</u>

"Play the book [title]."

"Read [title]."

"Play [title] from Audible."

Flash Briefing

"What's going on today?"

"What's new?"

"What's my Flash Briefing?"

Shopping

"Add [item name] to my cart."

"Order [item name]."

"Reorder [item name]."

"Cancel my order."

Weather and Traffic

"What's my commute?"

"What's the weather?"

"What's the traffic like right now?"

"Will it rain tomorrow?"

*To set up your location for traffic and weather, go to the *Fire TV* **Settings** menu, and from there, go to **Preferences > Location**.

Sports

"What was the score of the [team] game?"

"Did the [team] win?"

"When is the next [name of team] game?"

Local Venues

"What restaurants are nearby?"

"Find the business hours for [business establishment name]."

"What movies are playing at [theater name]?"

"When is the movie [title] playing today / tomorrow / this weekend / at [theater name]?"

"Tell me about the movie [title]."

<u>*Smart Home* Camera</u>

"Show [camera name]."

"Hide [camera name]."

How to Get Movies and TV Shows

Movies and TV shows can be purchased from *Prime Video*, and they can be accessed from other video services on the *Fire TV*.

1.) Go to the *Fire TV* menu and open **Movies** or **TV Shows**. You can also **Search** for a specific title.

Based on the apps installed on your device, you will see search results from *Prime Video* and other video services.

2.) Select a movie or TV show for the search results to view its details and purchase options. To see all options, select **More Ways to Watch**.

If a movie or TV show is available to view with another video app, such as *NETFLIX*, you can select that option to open the app and begin viewing from there. Be aware that some apps and providers do require additional authentications steps and subscription fees.

3.) Select **Buy** or **Rent** to purchase a movie or TV show from *Prime Video*. Then follow the on-screen instructions.

4.) Select **Watch Now** to start playback.

*You can watch movies and TV shows at no additional cost if you become an eligible *Amazon Prime* member. *Prime* members are allowed a one-month free trial. After the free trial expires, they pay a monthly or annual fee to watch unlimited *Prime*-eligible movies. The eligible movies will be in category rows labeled **Prime**.

How to Save Titles

To save titles in a customized list that you'd like to view later, select **Add to WATCHLIST** from the video details for a movie or TV show.

To delete a title from the WATCHLIST, select **Remove from WATCHLIST** in the details for a movie or TV show.

There are multiple ways to access the WATCHLIST:

• **From the computer:** Go to the *Prime Video* website and select **WATCHLIST** from the menu.

• **From the *Prime Video* app:** Select **WATCHLIST** from the menu.

• **From *Amazon Fire TV* devices:** Select **Your Videos** from the menu, then go to the **WATCHLIST** section.

How to Transfer Media to External Storage

If you'd like to free up space on your *Fire TV* device, media can be transferred to external storage.

Note: External storage options are not available for 3rd generation *Fire Stick* or *Fire TV* devices.

1.) Go to the *Amazon App Store.*

2.) Download and install ES File Explorer.

3.) Insert the Micro SD Card (for 2nd generation *Fire* TV) or USB drive (for 1st generation *Fire* TV) into the *Fire TV*.

4.) Look toward the lower-right corner of the screen and verify that the USB has been detected.

5.) Launch ES File Explorer. Select **Local** from the menu items list on the left side of the screen. Under **Local**, select the **Download** folder to view the items you'd like to transfer.

6.) Inside the **Download** folder, highlight the file(s) you'd like to transfer.

7.) Once the file is highlighted, press and hold the **Select** button on the remote. This should cause a check mark to appear on the file. You should also now be able to see a **Cut** option on the lower portion of the screen.

8.) Click the **Cut** option.

9.) Browse through the menu on the left side of the screen and locate the USB drive item. Depending on what type of drive you are using, it should say *USB* followed by some additional letters. Click it, then click **Open**.

10.) Click **Paste**.

How to Manage Apps

Most content can be managed directly from the *Fire TV*.

1.) Open **Settings** in the *Fire TV* menu.

2.) Go to **Applications**

3.) Go to **Manage Installed Applications**

Troubleshooting

Many issues can be resolved by restarting (unplugging the power cord and then plugging it back in) the device.

The device can also be restarted by using the remote. Press and hold the **Select** and **Play/Pause** buttons simultaneously for approximately five seconds. Or go to the *Fire TV* menu and select **Settings > Device > Restart**.

However, since restarting the device does not always solve every problem, here are some additional things to try.

Can only listen to *Prime Music* or *Amazon Music Unlimited Individual* plan on one device at a time

Trying to stream music on more than one device will bring up a notification that prompts you to switch the stream to your *Amazon Fire TV*.

This is due to a streaming limit.

Solution: Join the *Amazon Music Unlimited Family* plan, which allows you to stream on up to half a dozen devices per subscription.

Problem accessing external storage

*External storage is not available on 3rd generation *Fire TV*.

Solution: Safely remove the compatible storage device, then re-attach it to the *Fire TV*.

1.) Go to the *Fire TV* menu.

2.) Select **Settings > Device**.

3.) Select your storage device.

4.) Select **Eject**.

5.) Wait for the on-screen confirmation to pop up, then safely remove the device.

6.) Re-attach the storage device.

Forgotten PIN

Solution: Go to your *Prime Video Settings* on the *Amazon* website and reset the PIN.

1.) After going to your *Prime Video Settings*, go to the **Parental Controls** section.

2.) Look under **Prime Video PIN** and enter a new 5-digit PIN.

3.) Select **Reset Your PIN**

Issues with Audio

• Verify that the audio on the TV is not muted.

• If the *Fire TV* is connected to an AV receiver, verify that the receiver is on.

• 1.) Go to the *Fire TV* menu.

2.) Select **Settings**

3.) Go to **Display & Sounds**

4.) Go to **Audio**

5.) Verify that *DOLBY Digital Plus* is set to **Off**.

Issues with Display

• Adjust the video resolution or display configurations for your *Amazon Fire* TV.

1.) Go to the *Fire TV* menu.

2.) Select **Settings**

3.) Go to **Display & Sounds**

4.) Go to **Display**

5.) Select your preferred video resolution mode and calibrate your display.

• Calibrate the Display

1.) Go to **Settings** in the *Fire TV* menu.

2.) Go to **Display & Sounds**

3.) Go to **Display**

4.) Go to **Calibrate Display**

5.) Use the arrows to make the adjustments.

• If these steps do not resolve the issue, it might be beneficial to contact the TV manufacturer.

WI-FI Connectivity Issues

• Verify that the WI-FI password was entered correctly. Remember, passwords are case-sensitive.

• Verify that the router, modem, and/or network specifications meet the requirements for *Fire TV* devices.

Network Specification Requirements

- Open, WEP, WPA-PSK, and WPA2-PSK encrypted networks

- Hidden networks

Router/Modem Specifications

- B, G, and N routers on 2.4GHZ

- A and N routers on 5 GHZ

• Restart (unplug the power adapter, then plug back in) your *Fire TV* device

• Restart (unplug, then plug back in) your router/modem

• If you are using a Static IP address, go to **Settings > Network**. Then press **Select** and choose your IP address.

• If necessary, join your network using the WPS Button or PIN on your router or modem. Select **Settings > Network** from the *Fire TV* menu. Then choose the **Join Using WPS Button** or **Join Using WPS PIN** option.

• Check your internet connection by using the network status tool featured on the *Fire TV* device. To access the tool, select **Settings > Network** from the *Fire TV* menu, then press the **Play/Pause** button on your remote. Using this tool will help you diagnose connection issues while providing possible solutions.

• Move the *Fire TV* device away from electronics and other objects that can block your WI-FI signal.

• Verify that you are using the performance-optimizing power adapter included with your device.

• Verify that you are using the HDMI extender included with your *Fire TV* stick.

• If the issue persists, contact your Internet Service Provider, network administrator, or the manufacturer of your modem or router for assistance.

Difficulty Pairing the *Fire TV* App

• Verify that the mobile device you're using to download and install the *Fire TV* Remote App is compatible.

Fire TV Remote App is compatible with:

- *Fire* tablets with a microphone

- *Fire* phone

- *Android* devices (OS 4.0 or higher)

- IOS devices (7.0 or higher)

• Verify that your device has completed the app installation process

• If you're using another mobile device to mirror your display to your *Fire TV*, the *Fire TV* Remote App will not be able to pair. Stop mirroring on the other mobile device.

• Disconnect any remotes or accessories that you are not currently using from the *Fire TV*. Pairing management can be accessed by going to the *Fire TV* menu and selecting **Settings > Controllers & BLUETOOTH Devices**.

• If you are using an *Android* device, clear application data for the *Fire TV* Remote App.

1.) Open **Settings** for your device.

2.) Tap **Application Manager** or **Apps**.

3.) Select *Fire TV Remote App* from the list.

4.) Tap **Clear Data**.

5.) Tap **OK**.

6.) Re-open the *Fire TV* Remote App. Then try again to pair it to your device.

• If you are using a *Fire* phone, clear application data.

1.) Go to the **Home** screen and swipe downward to open the **Quick Actions** panel.

2.) Select **Settings**.

3.) Select **Manage applications**.

4.) Clear data.

Screen is Blank

• Verify that the TV is set to the same HDMI input channel your *Fire TV* is connected to.

• If you are using an HDMI cable to connect the *Fire TV* to your TV, disconnect it, then plug it back in.

• Try using a different HDMI cable.

• Temporarily disconnect other devices connected to your TV's HDMI ports.

• Change the TV to a different resolution. To illustrate, switch it from 1080p to 720p.

To change the resolution, press the **Up** and **Rewind** buttons on the *Fire TV* remote simultaneously for approximately five seconds. The system will begin cycling through various output resolutions. When you see a resolution that you'd like to switch to, select **Use Current Resolution**.

• If the *Fire TV* is connected to an AV receiver or soundbar, verify that the receiver is on and set to the correct input. If it still doesn't work, try connecting the *Fire TV* to the TV directly.

Fire TV Not Responding

• Verify that the batteries are inserted correctly with both positives pointing toward the top of the remote.

• Try pairing the controller or remote again.

1.) Remove and reinsert the batteries for the remote or controller.

2.) After the batteries are reinserted, the remote will automatically try to pair with the device.

3.) Wait for the on-screen message that confirms the remote has been discovered.

• If you are using an HDMI hub, disconnect the *Fire TV* device from the hub and plug it into the TV directly.

• Try using a different HDMI port on the TV.

• Verify that you are using the included power supply with the *Fire TV* device.

Difficulty Pairing *Fire TV* Remote or Game Controller

• Verify that the *Fire TV* remote and controller are compatible with the device.

Compatible remotes and controllers:

- *ALEXA* Voice Remote

- *Amazon Fire TV* Remote

- *Fire TV* Remote App

- *Amazon Fire TV* Game Controller

- USB and *BLUETOOTH* keyboards

- Some third-party wireless USB receivers and remotes

- Some third-party *BLUETOOTH* remotes

- Some third-party *BLUETOOTH* game controllers

• Turn off an actively connected remote or *BLUETOOTH* device that you are not currently using.

• Try to keep the remote within three meters of the *Fire TV* device.

• Move the *Fire TV* away from your TV and other electronics that can increase interference. Use the HDMI extender or adapter to keep the *Fire TV Stick* farther away from the TV.

• Pair the remote or controller again.

1.) Remove and reinsert the batteries for the controller or remote.

2.) After the batteries are reinserted, the remote will attempt to pair with the device automatically.

Difficulty Connecting *BLUETOOTH* Accessory to *Fire TV*

• Verify that the *BLUETOOTH* controller is compatible with *Fire TV Stick*

Compatible *BLUETOOTH* accessories:

- A2DP (Advanced Audio Distribution Profile)

- HID (Human Interface Device Profile)

- SPP (Serial Port Profile)

Note: *BLUETOOTH* headphones are not supported.

• Check network connection on the *Fire TV*

• Refrain from keeping the *Fire TV* in a cabinet

• Send the *Fire TV* into *Sleep* mode, then wake it up

• If the *BLUETOOTH* accessory was already paired to your *Fire TV*, re-pair it.

1.) Start by going to the *Fire TV* menu.

2.) Select **Settings**.

3.) Go to **Controllers and *BLUETOOTH* Devices**.

4.) Go to **Other *BLUETOOTH* Devices**.

5.) Select the previously paired device and press the **Menu** button on the *Fire TV* remote to remove it.

6.) Try pairing the *BLUETOOTH* accessory again.

• Verify that you are only pairing one *BLUETOOTH* accessory to the *Fire TV* at a time.

- For *Amazon Fire* devices, try switching to a wired connection if that's an option.

More From Emery H. Maxwell

Fire HD 10 Tablet Manual, available at all *Amazon* stores, including <u>U.S.</u>

Fire HD 8 Manual, available at all *Amazon* stores, including <u>U.S.</u>

Echo Dot Setup Instructions, available at all *Amazon* stores, including <u>U.S.</u>

PAPERWHITE User Guide, available at all *Amazon* stores, including <u>U.S.</u>